D0566263

WILD CATS

Cheetahs

Anne Welsbacher

ABDO Publishing Company

visit us at
www.abdopub.com

Published by Abdo Publishing Company 4940 Viking Drive, Edina, Minnesota 55435.
Copyright © 2000 by Abdo Consulting Group, Inc. International copyrights reserved in all
countries. No part of this book may be reproduced in any form without written permission
from the publisher.

Printed in the United States.

Photo credits: Peter Arnold, Inc.

Edited by Lori Kinstad Pupeza
Contributing editor Morgan Hughes

Library of Congress Cataloging-in-Publication Data

Welsbacher, Anne, 1955-
        Cheetahs / Anne Welsbacher.
        p. cm. -- (Wild cats)
        Includes index.
        Summary: Describes the physical characteristics, social, feeding, and hunting
        behavior, and life cycle of this swift African cat.
        ISBN 1-57765-087-5
        1. Cheetah--Juvenile literature. [1. Cheetah.] I. title. II. Series: Welsbacher, Anne,
        1955- Wild cats.
        QL737.C23W446   2000
        599.75'9--dc21   98-15727
                                                                            CIP
                                                                            AC

Contents

Wild Cats around the World

*T*he cheetah is a kind of wild cat. Cheetahs live mainly in Africa. Long ago, cheetahs lived in Asia and the Middle East, but many died. They were hunted by people and by lions. Many cheetahs were sick or could not have babies. Today, cheetahs are in danger of becoming **extinct**.

Cheetahs, like some other wild cats, have spots and stripes that help them blend in with the land around them.

All big cats have sharp claws. But cheetahs cannot pull their claws into their paws like other cats do. Their claws look like dog claws.

Each kind of big cat is good at something. Cheetahs are fast runners. They are the fastest animals in the world!

A pair of cheetahs in Africa.

Big Cat, Little Cat

Big cats are like house cats in many ways. Both big cats and little cats can see very well. Both lick themselves to keep clean.

Most big cats roar. But house cats do not roar. They purr. In this way, cheetahs are like house cats. They cannot roar, but they can purr.

Many big cats like to be alone. Some cheetahs do, too. But others like to be with other cheetahs.

This is true with house cats, too. Sometimes they like to be alone. Other times they want to be with other cats.

House cats lie with their tails curled up close. But most big cats stretch their tails out long. The cheetah has a long tail with black rings and bushy white fur at the end.

Cheetahs have good eyesight.

A Closer Look

Cheetahs are smaller than other wild cats. Including the tail, they are about as long as a grown-up person is tall. They weigh around 85 to 145 pounds (39 to 66 kg).

Cheetahs are different from most cats in other ways, too. They have bigger chests and smaller heads.

The cheetah cannot pull in its claws as other cats can. The claws grip the ground when the cheetah runs. They help it run fast!

The golden brown fur of a cheetah is rough. Its fur is covered with black spots the size of ping-pong balls. This coloring helps the fur blend in with tall grasses, hiding the cheetah from its enemies and its **prey**.

Cheetahs have long black marks from their eyes to their mouths. The marks look like teardrops. Black rings circle the tips of their tails.

Cheetahs have extra long, thick fur behind the neck. This fur is called a **mantle** or a mane. Cheetahs have long, slender legs. They have big, long teeth called **canine** teeth.

Cheetahs have long black marks from their eyes to their mouths.

The Cheetah at Home

Cheetahs live in flat, open grasslands where few trees and bushes grow. They like places where they can run! They don't live in forests. Cheetahs will hide in tall grass or climb trees to look for **prey**.

The areas that cheetahs live in are called their **habitats**. Cheetahs mostly live in Africa. They live in special parks that keep them safe. These parks are called **preserves**.

Cheetahs also live in zoos. Zoos are working to increase the number of cheetahs in the world.

Cheetahs climb trees to look for prey.

A Champion Runner

The cheetah is the fastest animal in the world. It can run 55 to 60 miles (88 to 97 km) per hour! That is the speed a car travels on the highway.

A cheetah can bolt into action very fast, too. It can go from 0 to 50 miles an hour (0 to 80 km an hour) in two seconds! That is faster than a car drives in the city.

Cheetahs cannot run at this speed for very long. In less than a minute, they must stop and rest.

Cheetahs have good sight. They can see an animal far, far away. They use their eyes to look for food. So cheetahs, unlike many wild cats, hunt during the daytime.

Many wild cats have certain places called their **territory**. They keep other cats out of their territory. Some cheetahs have well-defined territories. Other cheetahs travel a lot. Sometimes they don't claim a territory at all.

Adult cheetahs eat about six pounds (three kg) of meat a day. They can go without water for 10 days or even longer. They like to rest and nap in the daytime.

A cheetah was once recorded running 70 miles per hour (113 kmph).

The Predator's Prey

Cheetahs are **carnivores**. They also are called **predators**. The animals they eat are called **prey**.

Cheetahs eat gazelles, birds, rabbits, ostriches, wild pigs, and wildebeests. The animals they eat are smaller than the animals that other wild cats eat. Sometimes cheetahs eat fruit, too.

Cheetahs can run fast for only a few seconds. Then they must rest. So they try to get close to animals before they start to chase them.

Many cats, big and little, sneak up on their prey. But many times, the cheetah doesn't bother to do this. It gets close to an animal. Then it springs into full gallop!

The cheetah uses its front legs to knock the animal off its feet. Then it bites the animal's neck. It cuts off air, and the animal cannot breathe.

The cheetah drags its kill to a shady spot. It rests for a few minutes. Then it eats as fast as it can, before hyenas, vultures, or other animals steal its food.

A cheetah running down a gazelle.

Cat to Cat

Cheetahs live alone much of the time. But sometimes a male cheetah lives and hunts with one or more other male cheetahs. Many times, these cheetahs are brothers who stay together after they grow up.

When two or more cheetahs come together in this way, this is called a **coalition**. The coalition might last for a few days or as long as the cheetahs live.

Cheetahs sometimes fight with each other. A male will fight to protect a female. Females will fight to protect their babies, called cubs.

Cheetahs can be friendly with people, too. Long ago, people trained cheetahs to help them hunt. Today, some cheetahs in zoos can be near people without hurting them.

A coalition of cheetahs in an African preserve.

Cat Families

*F*emale cheetahs raise their cubs alone. The cheetah finds a hidden place in tall grasses, under a tree, or behind rocks. They usually give birth to three cubs.

Each cub is about one foot (.3 m) long, and weighs around eight pounds (four kg). The cubs are born with their eyes closed, and they cannot walk. Their fur is a fuzzy dark gray.

The fuzzy fur is long and thick. It makes the cubs look bigger than they are. This might help protect them from big animals looking for smaller animals to catch and eat.

The newborn cubs nurse their mother. But soon she must leave them to go hunting. Sometimes she is gone all day.

Cheetahs hunt every other day when they feed only themselves. But a mother cheetah must hunt every day to provide food for her cubs and herself.

Female cheetahs raise their cubs alone.

Growing Up

*A*bout one week after they are born, the cubs open their eyes and begin to crawl. Soon they grow teeth and begin to walk.

In four weeks, they can eat the meat their mother brings them. Soon she begins to teach them to hunt. She does not kill her **prey**. She brings it back alive and lets it loose. The cubs practice catching it!

Soon the cubs follow their mother on her hunting trips. She calls them with a chirping sound. If a cub gets lost, it chirps, too, and soon its mother finds it.

By the time they are about six months old, the cubs can help in the hunting. About this time, their fuzzy fur falls out and they begin to look like adult cheetahs.

When they are one year old, the young cheetahs hunt all by themselves. Soon, their mother leaves for good. It is time for them to be on their own.

Sometimes two or more of the cheetahs stay together. But other times each cheetah leaves to find its own place to live and hunt.

Wild cheetahs live around 13 years. Cheetahs that live in zoos can live about 15 years.

Cubs follow their mother on hunting trips.

Glossary

Canines—long, fanglike teeth that help kill prey.

Carnivore—an animal that eats meat.

Coalition—a group of two or more cheetahs that live and hunt together; a coalition might last for a few days, a few weeks, or as long as the cheetahs live.

Extinct—gone forever.

Habitat—the area and climate that an animal lives in.

Mantle—long, thick fur behind the neck of a cheetah, also called a mane. The long, thick fuzzy fur of a newborn cheetah cub is also called a mantle.

Predator—an animal that eats other animals.

Prey—an animal that is eaten by other animals.

Preserve—a special park where wild animals can live safe from hunting and other human activities.

Territory—an area or place where certain animals live; if others enter this area, the animal might fight or scare them off.

Internet Sites

Tiger Information Center
http://www.5tigers.org/
The Tiger Information Center is dedicated to providing information to help preserve the remaining five subspecies of tigers. This is a great site, with many links, sound, and animation.

The Lion Research Center
http://www.lionresearch.org/
Everything you want to know about lions is here. Lion research and conservation in Africa, information on lion behavior, and updates from researchers in the Serengeti about specific lion prides.

The Cheetah Spot
http://ThingsWild.com/cheetah2.html
This is a cool spot with sound and animation. Lots of fun information.

Amur Leopard
http://www.scz.org/asian/amurl1.html
This site links you to some great zoo spots. Very informative.

These sites are subject to change. Go to your favorite search engine and type in "cats" for more sites.

PASS IT ON

Tell Others What You Like About Animals!

To educate readers around the country, pass on interesting tips about animals, maybe a fun story about your animal or pet, and little-known facts about animals. We want to hear from you!

To get posted on the ABDO Publishing Company Web site, email us at "animals@abdopub.com"

Visit us at www.abdopub.com

Index